GHOST TOWNS
of the
AMERICAN WEST

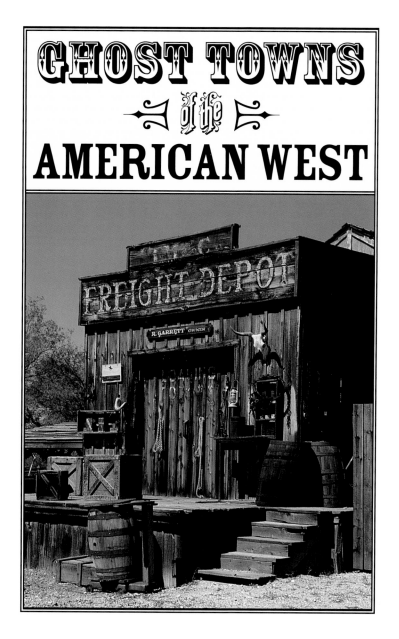

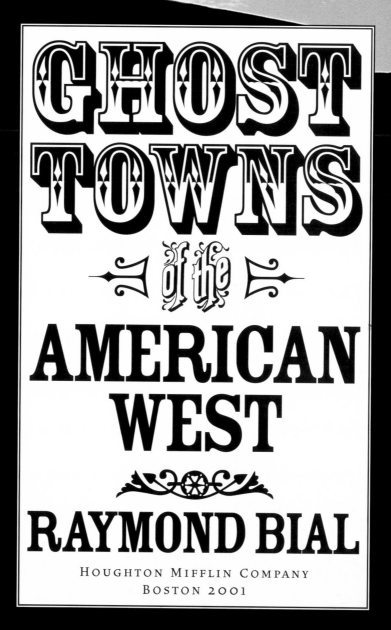

GHOST TOWNS

of the

AMERICAN WEST

RAYMOND BIAL

HOUGHTON MIFFLIN COMPANY
BOSTON 2001

To my wife, Linda, my children, Anna, Sarah, and Luke,

and my sister, Catherine, who helped in so many ways with this book.

— R.B.

The author would like to express his appreciation to the following locations in Arizona where most of the photographs in this book were made: Goldfield Ghost Town, Apacheland, and Old Tucson.

Visit our Web site: www.houghtonmifflinbooks.com.

Book design by Lisa Diercks
The text of this book is set in Vendetta Light and Rosewood.

Library of Congress Cataloging-in-Publication Data

Bial, Raymond.
Ghost towns of the American West / Raymond Bial.
p. cm.
ISBN 0-618-06557-1
1. Ghost towns — West (U.S.) — Juvenile literature. 2. West (U.S.) — History, Local — Juvenile literature. 3. Frontier and pioneer life — West (U.S.) — Juvenile literature. [1. Ghost towns. 2. West (U.S.) — History.] I. Title.
F591.B544   2001
978 — dc21
00-31895

Printed in Hong Kong
SCP 10 9 8 7 6 5 4 3 2 1

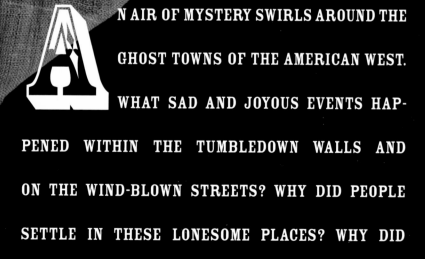

AN AIR OF MYSTERY SWIRLS AROUND THE GHOST TOWNS OF THE AMERICAN WEST. WHAT SAD AND JOYOUS EVENTS HAPPENED WITHIN THE TUMBLEDOWN WALLS AND ON THE WIND-BLOWN STREETS? WHY DID PEOPLE SETTLE IN THESE LONESOME PLACES? WHY DID

Ghost towns are rundown, but nothing seems out of the ordinary — until a shutter creaks open. It may simply be a wisp of wind, but perhaps a ghost is peering out from the velvety black rectangle of the window.

they pull up stakes and move away? What went wrong in these towns? Virtually every ghost town has untold stories of people who longed for a chance at a better life. Relics of the past, the towns now stand as evidence of high adventure, hopes of striking it rich, and the sudden loss of fortune — or life.

Under the bright sun of midday, dust blows around the gray buildings and tumbleweeds bounce eerily down the streets of many ghost towns. Windows with tattered curtains stare blankly upon the weathered boardwalk, hitching post, and abandoned water trough. At night, that plaintive *hoo-hoo* may be an owl nesting in a nearby saguaro cactus — or

Silhouetted against the deep blue of the evening sky, the buildings of this ghost town have long been deserted. Yet during the dark of night, they are filled with many unsettling sights and sounds.

the moaning of a restless ghost up in the graveyard. Maybe a young man was wrongly hanged as a horse thief or an unarmed cowboy was shot down in the saloon. Perhaps the moans rise from the soul of a lonely and unlucky prospector.

More than a few crusty and cantankerous old men with flowing white beards once wandered the mountains and deserts. With grub-stakes packed on their sturdy little burros, the old-timers had a gleam in their eyes — a gleam of gold and silver. Longing to strike it rich, they ventured forth into unknown and often dangerous territory. If they made a strike, others rushed after them to found a new town. Yet after years of misfortune, many prospectors simply gave up. There is a story about the Lost Dutchman, a prospector who couldn't find his way out of the Superstition Mountains of Arizona. To this day, it is believed that hikers disappear among the rocky crevices of those desert peaks, never to be seen again.

Any settlement abandoned by all or most of its inhabitants can be considered a ghost town. The ancient city of Pompeii, Italy, became a ghost town when the inhabitants were suddenly overwhelmed by lava from an eruption of Mount Vesuvius. Angkor, an ancient city in Cambodia, also became a ghost town. In North America, the ancient cliff dwellings in the desert Southwest became ghost towns when the Anasazi people moved to the Rio Grande Valley. The lost colony of Roanoke, founded by Sir Walter Raleigh along the Atlantic coast, can also be considered a ghost town, since the colonists mysteriously disappeared.

In America, settlers pushed westward over three centuries from the 1600s to the 1900s after the first English colonies were established along

Among the ghost towns in North America are the dwellings of the Pueblo Indians in the desert Southwest. Many of these buildings were constructed of handmade bricks known as adobe.

After several hard hours of travel, these trail-weary settlers paused in the foothills of the Rocky Mountains. Unhitching their wagon, they watered their livestock, ate a noonday meal, and briefly rested.

the Atlantic coast. They built new towns, only to move on after a few months or years. They left ghost towns throughout the nation, including the Midwest and the South. In fact, all fifty states, including Hawaii, have ghost towns. Historians estimate that there are about 30,000 abandoned towns scattered around the United States. Some experts believe that the number may be as high as 50,000 or more. Since the turn of the twentieth century, as more people moved to cities, many small rural communities have become ghost towns — and to this day farm towns are still dying out.

Although ghost towns can be found throughout the world, in the United States they are most often thought of as the mining camps, cowboy towns, and other settlements of the sprawling western frontier. Most were once mining camps where adventurous men came to seek their fortunes. These communities boomed as miners sought gold, silver,

Loading all of their possessions in Conestoga wagons with billowing canvas tops, settlers moved westward to homestead farms, stake a mining claim, or set up storekeeping in a new town.

Springing up throughout the West, towns quickly drew many inhabitants. For a while, everything appeared freshly painted and new — until the mines gave out or the cattle were driven to market elsewhere.

copper, or other precious minerals but died out when all of the ore was panned from streams or blasted from rocky tunnels. In cowboy towns, cattle were driven to other towns, then shipped to markets in the East. Many lumber camps in deep forests and farming communities on the broad prairies also enjoyed brief prosperity before they were abandoned. Along with the miners, cowboys, and farmers, merchants and bankers, as well as doctors and schoolteachers, also went west. They laid out streets and put up buildings in hopes of growth and prosperity. As one newspaper editor declared, most folks wished "to get rich if we can."

Western ghost towns — or traces of them — can be found from Texas to California and from Arizona to Montana and the Dakotas. There are

over 1,300 ghost towns in Nevada alone. Nearly as many towns flourished and faded in Montana, Colorado, New Mexico, and Utah. There are also many ghost towns in Oregon and Washington, along with Kansas, Nebraska, and other states of the Great Plains. The communities once prospered with gold or grain, wool or lumber, and other sources of wealth. However, many if not most of these ventures failed when the ore gave out in the mines or crops failed. Their hopes shattered, people moved away, leaving their homes and other buildings to the weather.

Today, most ghost towns are no more than abandoned sites where a town once stood in the lonely desert, high in the mountains, or somewhere on the thick carpet of prairie sod. They have vanished altogether,

Many western towns quickly attracted a large number of inhabitants. Other folks came to town on business, as evidenced in this photograph of the busy main street of Tonapah, Nevada, in 1903.

At the sites of many ghost towns, little is left — perhaps only a broken-down wagon once used to haul goods to market. The wooden wheels and sideboards gradually decay in the dry soil.

Most ghost towns were originally mining camps where men sought gold, silver, copper, and other precious minerals. Gold attracted swarms of miners first to California and later to the Black Hills of South Dakota.

and their locations have been found only through long hours of research and miles of hiking by determined historians. They are now nothing more than places, overgrown with grass and brush. Mark Twain, who went west to seek his fortune as so many other young men of the day did, described the state of a mining camp to which he returned twenty years later: "Not a single building, not a stick of wood, and sometimes not even foundation stones, at best only the faint outlines of the streets and building sites in the dust and grass." He said one would "find it hard to believe that there stood at one time a fiercely-flourishing

little city, of two thousand souls … and now nothing is left of it all but a lifeless, homeless solitude."

Other ghost towns are marked by a few ruins — a collapsed building, crumbling foundations, or an old mine shaft. Some ghost towns may still have reminders of days gone by: a handful of buildings, an abandoned mine, and a graveyard. One of the best-preserved ghost towns is Bodie, which is now protected as a state historic park in California. Bodie had a rough-and-ready history as a mining town during the California gold rush. Writing for *Harper's Monthly*, J. Ross Browne described the town as "a capital looking place for a den of robbers." During the winter, with snowdrifts as deep as twenty feet, one miner complained, "There's

Toward dusk, the glass panes in this window reflect the yellow warmth of the descending sun. Over time, the building will succumb to the weather — baking sun, intense rainstorms, and unforgiving winds.

A few adventurous people have sought their fortune not in gold and silver mines but in the ghost towns themselves. This "old-timer" has worked to restore Goldfield, Arizona, as a tourist attraction.

nothing to do, but hang around the saloons, get drunk and fight, and lie down in the snow and die." A story circulated about a woman, moving to town with her family, who prayed, "Good-by, God, we're going to Bodie." The *Bodie Free Press* later claimed unconvincingly that she had in fact cried, "Good, by God, we're going to Bodie."

Still other ghost towns are inhabited by a few *live* people. These diehard old-timers like the solitude or hope that boom times will again come their way. A handful of ghost towns had enterprising inhabitants who recognized that their communities appealed to sightseers. A cast of western characters had long been popular in fiction and film, and tourists wished to visit some of these haunts. Today, several ghost towns, including Tombstone, Arizona; Deadwood, South Dakota; Central City, Colorado; and Virginia City, Nevada, along with Calico and Nevada City, California, have been reborn as colorful tourist attractions. Today these towns have more visitors than ever.

Throughout the 1800s, hardy and resourceful settlers poured into the American West, starting thousands of little towns with an abiding hope for a better life. In 1840, Alexis de Tocqueville accurately described the restless spirit of the American who "builds a house in which to spend his old age and sells it before the roof is on." Yet some people objected to westward expansion. "What do we want with this vast, worthless area,

While its neighbor
Phoenix flourished,
Goldfield did so only
briefly, then declined
as a mining town.
However, the collection
of buildings has since
been given new life —
as a ghost town.

Rusting in the sun, this mine building has long since been abandoned. It's hard to imagine that not long ago, the place bustled with rough-and-tumble miners digging with picks and shovels.

this region of savages and wild beasts? I will not vote one cent from the public treasury to place the Pacific Ocean one inch nearer to Boston than it now is," Daniel Webster declared in 1838 — just eleven years before the California gold rush.

In 1849, James W. Marshall discovered gold at Sutter's Mill when he shut down the water on the millrace and glanced into the ditch. "I reached my hand down and picked it up; it made my heart thump for I felt certain it was gold," he recalled. Soon the word was out. "Gold! Gold!

Gold from the American River!" shouted Sam Brannon, waving a bottle of gold dust as he strode through the San Francisco streets. Seeking pay dirt, "forty-niners" (as the prospectors came to be known) streamed into California in the first of the great American gold rushes. Yet, over time, people came to refer to the sawmill as "Sutter's Folly" as the land of John Sutter was overrun with prospectors. Everywhere, men claimed "squatter's rights" in which they settled on land without paying for it.

Towns sprang up overnight. Charles B. Gillespie, a miner who worked near Coloma, California, described the typical main streets of these towns as "alive with crowds." To him, the miners were ragged, dirty men who were otherwise good-natured. They were a mix of Americans and immigrants — Germans, French, and other Europeans, and gold seekers from

Sometimes miners resorted to explosives, which they stored in a nearby shack, to blast away the rock.
They lived in shacks themselves, or in canvas tents pitched near their diggings.

China and Chile, along with British convicts from Australia. Mark Twain declared, "It was a driving, vigorous, restless population in those days … two hundred thousand *young* men — not simpering, dainty, kid-gloved weaklings, but stalwart, muscular, dauntless young braves, brimful of push and energy."

In 1851, when a Scottish artist named J. D. Borthwick arrived to try his luck as a prospector, he wrote that the main street of Hangtown, later renamed Pacerville, "was in many places knee-deep in mud, and was plentifully strewn with old boots, hats, and shirts, old sardine-boxes, empty tins of preserved oysters, empty bottles, worn-out pots and kettles, old

Hoping to strike it rich, miners hurried from one strike to another. Here, a group of men have set up a mining camp at a place known as Gregory's Diggings during the early days of the gold rush in Colorado.

ham-bones, broken picks and shovels, and other rubbish." Borthwick described the town as "one long straggling street of clapboard houses and log cabins, built in a hollow at the side of a creek, and surrounded by high and steep hills." Along the creek, he said, "there was continual noise and clatter, as mud, dirt, stones, and water were thrown about in all directions, and the men, dressed in ragged clothes and big boots, wielding picks and shovels . . . were all working as if for their lives."

Before long the California gold played out, but other strikes were made in Nevada, Montana, and elsewhere. Rushing to Colorado, miners cried, "Pike's Peak or Bust!" Newspaperman Horace Greeley, who visited

Coated with rust, old equipment is scattered around the mines — stamping machines used to crush rocks to get at the ore, carts that ran into the tunnels on "baby gauge" tracks just twenty inches wide, and other processing equipment.

Colorado in time for the gold rush in that region, noted that many miners "lost their hard earnings . . . and thousands who hasten hither will lay down to their long rest beneath the shadows of the mountains." Yet Greeley was so impressed by the prospect of instant wealth that he coined a popular phrase of the day, "Go west, young man!"

In the early months of their boom times, many towns lacked houses or even basic accommodations. When miners swarmed to San Pedro, New Mexico, a newspaper called the *Golden 9* advised them, "Bring a tent. If this is not possible, then bring along wagon sheets, canvas, table covers, door mats, gunny sacks, umbrellas, etc. with which to improvise

a tent-shack or tepee in which to live until you can make a dug-out or house … There are no vacant houses in town."

Within a few months, whether a mining camp or a cowtown, the community consisted of a ramshackle collection of buildings. Typically, townspeople raised buildings with whatever materials were available. Brick, plate glass, and even lumber might be hundreds of miles away and might take weeks to be shipped. So folks put up buildings of local stone or, out on the prairies, they laid down slabs of sod. In the desert, the main street might be lined with adobe buildings. In the forests of Idaho and Colorado, people built log stores and houses. Yet as soon as lumber

Some communities grew into bustling towns, while many others were abandoned. Ghost towns may not be inhabited by restless spirits whose lives ended in heartbreak and tragedy, but a haunting atmosphere pervades Main Street.

*The men who poured
into the new towns
looked forward to
a bath and a bed, but
accommodations weren't
always the best. J. Ross
Browne recalled that the
floors of one Virginia
City hotel "were covered
from the attic to the
solid earth — three
hundred human beings
in a tinder-box not
bigger than a first-class
hen-coop!"*

became available through a local sawmill or wagon shipment, the make-shift structures were replaced by frame buildings.

With few skilled craftsmen on the frontier, people didn't worry much about style. Often the buildings simply featured a false front, an outside staircase to the second floor, and a roofed portico, a kind of open porch, which offered shelter to passers-by. Left unpainted, buildings weathered to a light gray. The raised wooden sidewalk in front kept people's feet safely above the dust or the knee-deep mud. Main Street was usually broad, since teams of horses and wagons needed a great deal of space. People built wood-frame houses on the side streets.

Among the important business establishments were the saloon, the

Most of the rectangular buildings had wooden false fronts to make them appear large and grand on the dusty frontier. Among the most important enterprises was the mercantile store, which offered a wide variety of goods.

hotel, boarding houses, and, in mining towns, the assay office, where ore was tested to see if it held gold or other valuable minerals. At the heart of retail enterprise was the general store, which offered merchandise to satisfy just about every need: sugar and salt, molasses and meat, gunpowder and ammunition, as well as coffee and cloth. In time, the community might have a drugstore, barber shop, meat market, restaurant, and maybe even a photography studio.

By August 1864, Virginia City, a mining town in the wilds of Montana, had acquired a newspaper, the *Montana Post*, which reported, "Though our city is but a year old, fine and substantial buildings have been erected and others are going up . . . Indeed, the whole [town] appears to be a work of magic . . . the vision of a dream." Miners, however, most often entertained

themselves with a few shots of whiskey in the local saloon — most towns had numerous drinking establishments. Like most western towns, Virginia City, Nevada, sought to become a "steady business city," yet it was reported that there was a saloon "every fifteen feet."

Perhaps the most famous resident of Virginia City was Mark Twain. He and a partner staked a claim to a silver mine, about which he recalled, "We put our name to it and tried to feel that our fortunes were made." Like most prospectors, however, Twain never found silver or gold. Making a name for himself as a newspaper writer, he recalled the bustling growth of Virginia City: "Large fire-proof buildings were going up in the principal streets, and the wooden suburbs were spreading out in all directions. Town lots soared up in prices that were amazing."

Most remaining ghost towns are in the West, where the dry climate preserved their wood structures. Many of these towns also sprang up on open public land.

Some mining towns relied on placer deposits, where gold was panned from a nearby stream. When all of the gold was washed from the sand or gravel, the town quickly died. If the mining went to the "hard rock" stage, in which chunks of ore were mined, the town flourished a while longer, until the vein was "pinched out," meaning all the ore had been dug. The miners then rushed to seek their fortunes elsewhere. It seemed that precious minerals were being found throughout the West. In 1874, Colonel George Armstrong Custer stumbled upon gold in the Black Hills of present-day South Dakota, and prospectors swarmed into the land held sacred by the Sioux.

Within a year, Deadwood, South Dakota, became a boomtown of

about 25,000 people. Of course, no one was ever certain of the exact population. As one of the inhabitants wrote, "You can't count people living in layers." Among those who came to Deadwood were many colorful people. It was reported that one woman in town regularly smoked cigars and could beat anyone at poker, but devoutly refused to do so on Sundays. However, the most famous people in town were Martha Jane Canary, better known as Calamity Jane, and James Butler Hickock, known to friend and foe alike as Wild Bill Hickock.

Renowned scout, buffalo hunter, and soldier, Wild Bill was the most notorious "shootist," or gunfighter, of the day. No one dared to stand up to him. It would have been "suicide," explained Crooked Nose Jack

The town of Goldfield, Arizona, was abandoned long ago — but then someone lights a lantern in an upstairs room, reminding us that a few people still live in some ghost towns.

Mine "workings" were
either tunnels braced
with wooden timbers or
open pits. Often, entire
hillsides were eaten away
and the rock pulverized
by this equipment before
miners moved on to
other promising sites.

McCall, who tracked Hickock down in Deadwood. McCall wanted to make a name for himself by killing the legendary gunfighter. As Wild
Bill played cards, McCall shot him in the back
of the head. Wild Bill was holding all aces and
eights, which has since been called a "dead man's
hand." The undertaker who prepared the remains
for burial described Wild Bill as "the prettiest
corpse I have ever seen." Among the mourners
was Calamity Jane. She was acclaimed throughout the West not only for stirring up trouble but
for helping people in need. After leaving home as
a young girl for a wild life on the frontier, she
caroused with miners, cowboys, and gunslingers
for many years. She also nursed the sick and
comforted the dying.

Like mining communities, cattle towns had more than a few saloons
for cowboys, gamblers, and outlaws along with other Main Street enterprises. The merchants in Dodge City, Kansas, one of the rowdiest frontier towns of the West, certainly liked the cowboys who freely spent their
money in the saloons and stores on Front Street — but not their reckless
fighting. In the typical western town, the buildings were often skirted
with a sidewalk of wooden planks, along with hitching posts and water
troughs for horses. There might be a bank made of solid brick to assure
depositors that their hard cash or gold dust was safe from robbers. There
might also be a mercantile store, an early version of the department store,

*Every town had its Boot
Hill, so named because
the men buried there
usually died with their
boots on. Each grave
mound was marked
with a wooden cross or
rough board on which
was scrawled the name
of the deceased.*

Cattle towns, in particular, relied on the local blacksmith shop and livery stable. Here, horses could be shoed and boarded while people were in town for business or pleasure.

as well as a general store. The town certainly had to have a blacksmith shop and livery stable, as well as corrals for horses and cattle. Some towns had a telegraph office and their very own newspaper. The town might be lucky enough to be on a stagecoach route, a Pony Express station, or, better yet, a railroad stop.

"The Americans have a perfect passion for railroads," wrote Michel Chevalier, a French economist, in the 1830s. If the railroad bypassed the village, it quickly became a ghost town. Helen Hunt Jackson described Garland City, Colorado, where she lived: "Twelve days ago there was not a house here. Today, there are one hundred and five, and in a week there will be two hundred." However, the town lasted only a few months, at

Many towns became centers for trade and communications. Along with the stagecoach and telegraph office, they might also have a depot for freight wagons — at least until the railroad came through town.

Over time, people became fascinated by the dangers of the West. Anyone who was willing to take a chance could have a better life on the frontier — especially when movie heroes like John Wayne brought law and order to the dusty streets.

least at that site. When the railroad passed thirty miles to the west, folks moved the entire town — walls and windows, as well as sidewalks, furnishings, and goods — to the railroad tracks. Railroads laid down thousands of miles of gleaming tracks across the grasslands, with a transcontinental link completed in 1869.

Decent towns also had a sheriff's office and jail, often with a nearby gallows casting a long shadow down the street. Back east, these kinds of towns became the subject of widely read paperbacks known as "dime novels," which glorified the gunfighters and gamblers. Later, Westerns became popular as movies and television shows. These "shoot-'em-ups"

"Wanted" posters were tacked onto buildings in towns throughout the West, and many men achieved fame not for their good deeds but for the number of other men they had killed, often in cold blood.

Seldom a fancy building, the sheriff's office nonetheless occupied a prominent location on Main Street. It often included a sturdy jail, where desperadoes could be held until they came before a judge (if they were lucky enough to have a trial).

portrayed a Wild West in which there was no law except that of the gun. Much was myth, but not all of the legends were invented. Mark Twain recalled the wanton violence of Virginia City: "If a man wanted a fight on his hands without any annoying delay, all he had to do was to appear in public in a white shirt or stove-pipe hat, and he would be accommodated."

Similarly, according to a local reporter, people were safe in Sheridan, Wyoming, as long as they minded their own business: "Delicate inquiries into matters which belong to your neighbor are not healthy." A law-abiding man in Newton, Kansas, about twenty-five miles north of

Western justice was swift and certain. Most every town had its gallows, silhouetted against the deepening sky. Here, many a murderer and horse thief climbed the steps to the platform to meet his fate.

Undertakers and gravediggers made a good livelihood by burying the dead. Skilled carpenters might also earn a little extra money by hammering together crude wooden coffins.

Wichita, noted that saloons accounted for much of the town's size. Guns were constantly fired, reminding him of a Fourth of July celebration: "There was shooting when I got up and shooting when I went to bed."

There were many outlaws, bandits, and desperadoes swaggering down the streets of these towns — Billy the Kid, Jesse James, and many others. For better or worse, each achieved fame for his quick draw, mean streak, and death at a young age. Among the worst of the bunch was Henry Plummer, who once claimed, "I'm too wicked to die." He was hanged anyway. Law and order had to be brought to what became known as the Wild West,

but guns blazed in the meantime. In Nevada City, California, a group of vigilantes caught up with one culprit who had been sentenced to be hanged. As they were bringing the outlaw back to town, he said, "I'll bet you fifty dollars that my horse can outrun any horse in this posse." Being good sports, the men in the posse could not resist the challenge, and the outlaw galloped away. It took two hours to catch him, but a rope was soon around his neck and his limp body was swaying in the breeze.

It required tough men to bring peace and justice to the West. When Jack Slade became a law officer for the Overland Stage Line in the 1860s, Mark Twain noted, "The outlaws soon found that the new agent was a man who did not fear anything that breathed the breath of life ... Slade had to

"Someday you'll find your tombstone," soldiers warned one old prospector who ventured too often into Apache country. Hutch Stevens recalled in The Restless Longing: A Prospector's Story, *"A prospector lives in hopes, and dies in some old cabin."*

kill several men — some say three, others say four, and others six — but the world was the richer for their loss." Yet over time, Slade began to run wild, killing whomever he pleased. Slade "might often be seen galloping through the streets, shouting, yelling, firing revolvers," according to Thomas J. Dimsdale, who lived in Virginia City. Eventually, Slade was sentenced to be hanged by the neck until dead. Dimsdale reported, "Everything being ready, the command was given, 'Men, do your duty,' and the box being instantly slipped from beneath his feet, he died almost instantaneously."

Of all the towns that sprang up in the West, one became most noto-

rious for its frequent violence and sudden death. Even its name spoke of the ultimate hazard of living there — Tombstone. In this parched Arizona town just east of Tucson, the local newspaper was appropriately named the *Epitaph*. As a newspaperman explained at the time, "What is Tombstone without an Epitaph?" Tombstone became famous as the home of John Henry "Doc" Holliday, Frank Leslie, and the Earp Brothers, as well as a host of other short-tempered men with itchy trigger fingers.

Up on Boot Hill, the tombstone of Bob Heath briefly described his death at the hands of residents of nearby Bisbee, Arizona: "Taken from County Jail and lynched by Bisbee mob in Tombstone, Feb. 22, 1884." Another grave simply listed the dead and noted the proper manner in which they were "LEGALLY Hanged, March 8, 1884." One of the most

The shootout at the O.K. Corral became one of the most celebrated — and hotly disputed — acts of violence in the settling of the West. It is doubtful that anyone will ever know the whole story of what happened that fateful day.

Creaking idly in the wind, late at night, this lantern hangs near the entrance of an old saloon. Its yellow glow seems to cast more shadows than light, making one wonder just what is out there in the dark.

humorous epitaphs, though not for the man who was gunned down, is the following:

HERE LIES LESTER MOORE FOUR SLUGS FROM A .44 NO LESS, NO MORE.

Of all the deadly acts in Tombstone, and possibly the entire West, the shootout at the O.K. Corral on October 26, 1881, became the most famous. In this gunfight, the Earp brothers killed several men of the so-called Clanton clan. No one knows for sure what happened on that fateful day. Just after the incident, curious citizens went over to the O.K. Corral and clumsily trampled the evidence. The next morning the *Epitaph* reported: "The feeling of the better class of citizens is that the Marshal and his posse acted solely in the right in attempting to disarm the cowboys and that it was a case of kill or be killed." Others accused the Earp brothers of "wanton murder." The Earps were acquitted, but folks in Tombstone remained so bitterly divided by the killings that President Chester A. Arthur threatened to impose martial law in 1882. Tombstone could never be considered a good, safe place to raise a family. To this very day, people continue to debate whether the Earps acted in self-defense or gunned down the cowboys in cold blood.

*Inside this home,
the walls and furniture
are whitened with dust
and cobwebs. Broken
chairs and tables, along
with a few cans and jars,
may be the only signs
that someone lived
here long ago.*

None of these towns would have prospered, even briefly, and the frontier would never have become settled, without women and children.
Storekeepers and farmers occasionally brought their wives and children
with them, but men still outnumbered women nine to one. Most towns

A MINERS HOME IN COLORADO

Women were needed in the West, especially those with a spirit of independence. This miner constructed a rough log home for his wife and daughter, who accompanied him into the mountains of Colorado.

actively sought women. In 1860, a letter to the editor of the *Rocky Mountain News* from the new settlement of Breckenridge, Colorado, read: "A few very respectable looking women have ventured over to see us. Send us a few more." Another Colorado writer asked, "We have one lady living in Breckenridge and one on Gold Run; we would be glad to welcome many arrivals of the 'gentler' portion of the gold-seeking humanity, and can offer a pleasant country, good locations, and peaceable neighbors . . . except for an occasional lawsuit."

The waves of western migration reached a peak between 1860 and 1880. Over time, some towns grew into large cities, such as Denver and

Phoenix, while many others were abandoned and forgotten in the desert sands or mountain snows. Most went bust because of economic failure — all the gold or silver was mined or the cattle were driven to another market town. A few people got rich, but others suffered heartbreak, hunger, and plain bad luck, then abandoned the town. Perched on mountain cliffs, tucked into a wooded valley, or baking in the desert sun, these ghost towns are so remote that they are almost impossible to find. People often have to travel to them by four-wheel-drive vehicles and then hike several miles up rocky slopes or over cactus-studded deserts. Finding the ghost towns may be as difficult as the search for gold that led to the founding of the towns.

John Steele described Washington, California, in the 1840s, just six months after it had been founded: "With a large number of vacant cabins

All that is left of many homes in Goldfield, a turn-of-the-century ghost town in Arizona, are a few concrete foundation slabs. Gradually, even these faint vestiges are being taken over by cacti and drifting sand.

it contained several empty buildings and quite a large hotel, closed and silent." Once ringing with the voices of cheerful people, the towns have now fallen silent. They have become little more than empty shells of their former selves. There may be a handful of old false-front buildings, weathered to

a haunting gray, with open doorways and broken windows. But little else remains; few people even remember the place. Even the memories, along with the hopes and dreams of the inhabitants, have blown away, like so much dust in the wind.

FURTHER READING

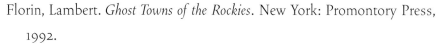

Florin, Lambert. *Ghost Towns of the Rockies*. New York: Promontory Press, 1992.

———. *Ghost Towns of the West*. New York: Promontory Press, 1993.

Lawliss, Chuck. *Ghost Towns, Gamblers and Gold*. New York: W. H. Smith Publishing Co., 1985.

Living Ghost Towns. New York: Crescent Books, 1986.

McCoy, Michael. *The Wild West: A Traveler's Guide*. Old Saybrook, Conn.: Globe Pequot Press, 1995.

Miller, Donald C. *Ghosts on a Sea of Grass: Ghost Towns of the Plains: Colorado, Kansas, Montana, Nebraska, New Mexico, North Dakota, Oklahoma, South Dakota, Texas, Wyoming*. Missoula, Mont.: Pictorial Histories Publishing Co., 1990.

O'Neal, Bill. *Ghost Towns of the American West*. Lincolnwood, Ill.: Publications International, 1995.

Robotham, Tom. *Ghost Towns: How They Were Born, How They Lived, and How They Died*. Philadelphia: Courage Books, 1993.

Sagstetter, Beth. *The Mining Camps Speak: A New Way to Explore the Ghost Towns of the American West*. Denver, Colo.: BenchMark Publishing of Colorado, 1998.

Silverberg, Robert. *Ghost Towns of the American West*. Athens: Ohio University Press, 1994.

Speck, Gary B. *Dust in the Wind: A Guide to American Ghost Towns*. Sweet Home, Ore.: White's Electronics, 1996.

Topping, Gary. *Ghost Towns of the Old West*. New York: Mallard Press, 1992.

Wheeler, Keith. *The Townsmen*. New York: Time Life Books, 1975.

CHILDREN'S BOOKS

Burt, Olive Woolley. *Ghost Towns of the West*. New York: J. Messner, 1976.

Stone, Lynn M. *Ghost Towns*. Vero Beach, Fla.: Rourke Publications, 1993.